Contents

Delicious India

India is part of the continent of Asia. Enormous mountains called the Himalayas are in the north of India. They are the highest mountain range in the world. The huge River Ganges, which is 2,505 km long, begins in the Himalayas. India also has desert and tropical forests.

The national animal of India is the Bengal tiger and the national flower is the lotus flower. There is even a modern temple in New Delhi called the Lotus Temple. Indians think food is very important and the country even has a national fruit, the mango.

People from different religions eat different foods in India. For example, Hindus do not eat beef and Muslims do not eat pork. Many people in India do not eat meat at all. Most dishes are freshly made using vegetables, herbs and a lot of spices. Rice and bread are served at most meals.

The Lotus Temple in New Delhi is shaped like a lotus flower.

The River Ganges is important to Hindus. There are sacred sites on the river's banks.

Delicious curries are one of the most popular Indian foods.

Get Ready to Cook

Cooking is fun! There's nothing better than making food to share with your family and friends.

Every recipe page in this book starts with a 'You will need' list. This is a set of ingredients. Make sure you collect everything on the list before you start cooking.

Look out for the 'Top tips' boxes. These have great tips to help you cook.

'Be Safe!' boxes warn you when you need to be extra careful.

Use one chopping board for meat and fish and a different chopping board for vegetables and fruit.

Always ask a grown-up if you can do some cooking.

Watch out for sharp knives! Ask a grown-up to help you with chopping and cutting.

Make sure you wash your hands before you start cooking.

Always wash any fruit and vegetables before using them.

Wear an apron to keep your clothes clean as you cook.

Always ask a grown-up for help when cooking on the hob or using the oven.

West Bengal

The area of West Bengal is found at the top of the Bay of Bengal. West Bengal is on the border with Bangladesh and its capital city is Calcutta. It lies on the banks of the River Hugli and was once the capital of India when Britain ruled the country.

Bengali cooking

Bengalis eat a lot of rice, lentils, fish and vegetables. Sometimes they wrap fish in pumpkin leaves to cook them. They use coconut in their dishes, and a lot of spices to bring out the flavour of their food. Some dishes are mild and some are quite spicy.

Sweet treats

Sweets and desserts, called *mishti*, are popular in Bengal. Bengalis make delicious sweets using cottage cheese. These include *chanar payesh*, which is made with pistachio nuts and cardamom. Bengalis love *sandesh*, which is a dish that is served at the end of a meal. It is a bit like a milk jelly and is flavoured with almonds and saffron.

Fish wrapped in pumpkin leaves is one of the tasty dishes eaten in West Bengal.

Street vendors make fresh juices to order. So delicious!

Pantua are balls of cottage cheese and milk that are fried. They are a popular dessert.

Aloo Ka Paratha

You will need:

5 medium-sized potatoes, peeled, boiled and mashed
2 tsp ground coriander
1 tsp ground cumin
½ tsp cumin seeds
½ tsp ground turmeric
1 tsp chilli powder
salt, to taste
3 tbsp fresh coriander, finely chopped
5 cm piece of fresh root ginger, finely grated
250 g plain flour
2 tbsp vegetable oil
water, to mix

These tasty flatbreads are stuffed with mashed potato and seasoned with spices and other flavourings. *Parathas* are eaten for breakfast in India, with chutneys and pickles. You can also eat them with yoghurt.

BE SAFE!
• Ask a grown-up to help you prepare the potatoes.
• Watch out for your fingers when you are grating the fresh ginger.

Step 1

In a bowl, mix the mashed potato with the spices, salt, coriander and ginger. Put aside.

Step 2

Put the flour and vegetable oil in a mixing bowl. Rub together until the mixture is crumbly. Add water, a little at a time. Knead well to make a dough. Cover with a clean tea towel and put aside for 1 hour.

Step 3

Divide the dough into pieces about the size of golf balls. Flatten the balls into circles. Then spoon some potato mixture into the centres. Fold the edges of the circles in over the potato and pat to flatten.

Step 4

Heat a griddle pan and cook the parathas. Place in the pan and flip when you start to see bubbles. Oil the paratha then flip again. Oil the other side and flip. Continue until crisp and golden on both sides.

TOP TIP You could use wholemeal flour, if you prefer, for your parathas.

Punjabi Tastes

The state of Punjab is in the north-west of India. Its name means 'Land of Five Waters' because the state has five rivers. A lot of farming takes place in Punjab because the soil there is so rich and the supply of river water makes it easy to water crops.

Punjabi food

Punjabis like rich food. Milk, butter and cream are used in most dishes. Both wheat and corn are grown in Punjab and made into a lot of different kinds of bread. Tandoori roti, naan, parathas and *kulcha* are all popular, especially stuffed parathas. In Punjab, people eat rice only at very special meals, such as wedding or birthday celebration meals.

Spicy mixtures

Punjabi cooks use a lot of onion, garlic, fresh ginger and tomatoes in their cooking. They also like to use spices. This is why so many of their dishes are called 'masala', which means 'a spicy mixture'. Spices used include coriander seeds, cumin and cloves. Punjabi people also cook with black pepper, red chilli and mustard. These spices make the food taste very hot. Turmeric is used to add an earthy flavour and a lovely yellow colour to dishes.

The Golden Temple at Amritsar is one of the most famous places in Punjab.

Street vendors cook and sell tasty breads on the pavements and in the markets of Punjab cities.

13

Rajma

You will need:

2 tbsp sunflower oil
1 tsp cumin seeds
2 onions, finely chopped
5 cm piece of fresh
  root ginger
6 garlic cloves, crushed
2 large tomatoes, chopped
  into 2.5 cm cubes
2 fresh green chillies,
  finely chopped
2 tsp ground coriander
1 tsp ground cumin
¼ tsp ground turmeric
1 tsp garam masala
2 400 g tins kidney beans
salt, to taste

This vegetarian curry is a favourite in Punjabi cooking. Kidney beans are cooked with onions, tomatoes and spices. *Rajma* goes well with boiled rice and is a great, spicy dish to try on a cold, wintry day.

BE SAFE!
- Be careful when opening the tins.
- Ask a grown-up to help with the chopping.

Step 1

Heat the oil in a pan and add the cumin seeds. When they start sizzling, add the onion and sauté. Add the ginger and garlic and sauté for 2 minutes.

Step 2

Now add the green chillies, tomatoes, ground coriander, cumin, turmeric and garam masala. Then sauté, stirring, until the oil separates from the mixture.

Step 3

Drain and rinse the kidney beans. Add to the pan with 750 ml warm water and add salt to taste. Cook until the beans are very soft (around 10 minutes). Mash the beans slightly to thicken the sauce.

Step 4

Serve the rajma hot with rice and perhaps a cucumber salad and your favourite pickled vegetable.

TOP TIP Cook this dish the day before you want to eat it. Leave it overnight and it will taste even better!

Beautiful Kerala

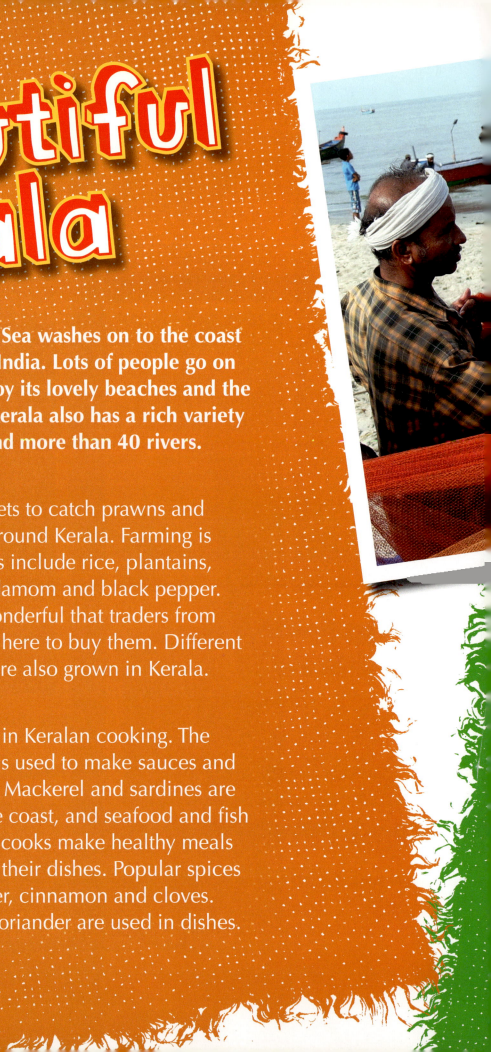

The beautiful Arabian Sea washes on to the coast of Kerala in south-west India. Lots of people go on holiday to Kerala to enjoy its lovely beaches and the warm, sunny weather. Kerala also has a rich variety of plants and animals and more than 40 rivers.

Fishing and farming

Fishermen use large nets to catch prawns and fish in the shallow sea around Kerala. Farming is also important and crops include rice, plantains, coconuts, cashews, cardamom and black pepper. Keralan spices are so wonderful that traders from all over the world come here to buy them. Different types of tea and coffee are also grown in Kerala.

Cooking in Kerala

Coconut is often used in Keralan cooking. The flesh is grated, the milk is used to make sauces and coconut oil is used, too. Mackerel and sardines are cooked every day on the coast, and seafood and fish are often eaten. Keralan cooks make healthy meals and use lots of spices in their dishes. Popular spices include cumin, coriander, cinnamon and cloves. Fresh curry leaves and coriander are used in dishes.

16

Fishermen pull their nets on to the beach. They will mend them before they go out for another catch.

Locally caught fish are used to make delicious Keralan dishes.

17

Lassi

You will need:

$\frac{1}{8}$ tsp saffron threads

1 425 g tin of sliced mango/
   mango pulp or
   1 large fresh mango

500 ml plain yoghurt

150 ml milk or unsweetened
   condensed milk

30 g caster sugar

300 g crushed ice

This is a yoghurt-based Indian drink. It can be savoury or sweet. On a very hot day, lassi is a great way to quench your thirst. Sweet varieties use many different fruits.

BE SAFE!
- If you are using tinned mango, be careful when opening the tin.
- Ask a grown-up to operate the blender.

Step 1

Using a pestle and mortar, grind the saffron threads until they turn into a powder. Pour in about half of the milk or condensed milk and stir until well combined.

Step 2

If you are using a fresh mango, ask a grown-up to halve it and then make vertical and horizontal cuts on the mango halves. Press on the skin side so the halves look like little orange porcupines!

TOP TIP If the mixture in the blender is too stiff, add some water.

Step 3

Peel off the squares of mango with your fingers or use a small, sharp knife. Then carefully cut the remaining flesh from around the pit.

Step 4

Put the mango pieces or pulp, plain yoghurt, the remaining milk or condensed milk, sugar, crushed ice and the ground saffron mixture in a blender.

Step 5

Blend for about two minutes. The mixture should become smooth and creamy. Pour into tall glasses to serve.

Rich Rajasthan

The state of Rajasthan is in the north-west of India, next to Pakistan. It is hilly in the south-east and a desert called the Thar Desert is in the north-west. Many different tribes live in Rajasthan. Some of them wear bright clothes and lots of jewellery.

Taste of Rajasthan

Rajasthanis cook using ghee. This is butter that has been boiled. It can sometimes be hard to find water in Rajasthan, so people often use milk instead of water to cook. Rajasthanis do not cook many fresh green vegetables because it is hard to grow plants in this part of India. Instead, they eat lentils and beans. They also love sweet dishes, which are served before the main course.

Spicy chutney

A chutney is a sauce made of pickled fruits and spices. Pickled foods, such as fruits and vegetables, are preserved in vinegar or brine. Chutneys are flavoured with spices and sugar. Rajasthani chutneys use turmeric, coriander seed, mint and garlic.

Rajasthani markets have a lot of lentils and beans for sale.

Colourful cooking spices are sold in Rajasthani markets.

Chicken Biryani

This dish is often served on special occasions. The raisins in it give the chicken a sweet taste. The dish also contains whole spices. Don't eat them, though! They are used just to give the food a tasty flavour.

You will need:

225 g basmati rice
2 tbsp butter
1 large onion, finely sliced
1 bay leaf
3 cardamom pods
1 small cinnamon stick
1 tsp ground turmeric
4 skinless, boneless chicken
    breast fillets, cubed
4 tbsp curry paste
125 g raisins
875 ml chicken stock
spring onions,
    finely sliced,
    to garnish

BE SAFE!

- Use separate chopping boards for vegetables and meat.
- Ask a grown-up to slice the onion.

Step 1

Put the rice in a large colander and rinse under cold running water until the water runs clear. Put aside.

Step 2

Heat the butter in a large pan. Cook the onions with the bay leaf, cardamom pods and cinnamon stick for 10 minutes, stirring occasionally. Stir in the turmeric. Add the chicken and curry paste. Cook until the chicken is no longer pink and the juices run clear.

Step 3

Stir the rice into the pan. Add the raisins and pour in the stock. Cover the pan with a lid and bring to the boil. Lower the heat and cook for 10 minutes. Now turn off the heat and leave for another 10 minutes.

Step 4

Garnish with the spring onions and then serve while hot.

TOP TIP You can buy curry paste in most supermarkets.

Delhi Delights

Delhi is an area in central north India. It includes India's capital city, New Delhi, which is found on the banks of the River Yamuna.

Old Delhi

Old Delhi was once India's capital city. It is made up of many narrow lanes. There are a lot of old *haveli* (brightly decorated houses), mosques and bazaars here. Chandni Chowk is a huge market area where people sell food, spices, clothes, shoes and many more items.

Fantastic flavours

The wealthy people of Delhi can choose just about any style of cooking they like. There are hundreds of restaurants in the capital city. Some cook Indian food, some make Asian foods and others serve up Western-style dishes.

Street food

Food stalls can be found everywhere in the city. The most common street food is *chaat*, which are savoury snacks. They include deep-fried pastries and stuffed breads. *Kulfiwalas* are street sellers who serve delicious ice creams.

Street food and street markets are found all over Delhi. These street vendors are selling fresh vegetables.

City pavements are filled with spicy snacks for sale.

Sesame Cookies

You will need:

500 g plain flour
pinch of salt
¼ tsp bicarbonate of soda
125 g caster sugar
225 g butter, at room
　　temperature, diced
3 eggs
1 tbsp caraway seed
60 g sesame seeds
120 ml milk

These little cookies are simple and fun to make. They are a healthy option, too! The sesame and caraway seeds give the cookies a lovely, nutty flavour. They taste delicious as an after-dinner treat or as a sweet snack.

BE SAFE!
• Ask a grown-up to help you use the oven.
• Always use oven gloves.

Step 1

Preheat the oven to 180°C. Grease a baking tray. Sieve the flour with the salt and bicarbonate of soda into a mixing bowl. Add the sugar, butter, 2 eggs and the caraway seeds, then mix the ingredients.

Step 2

Stir in the milk a bit at a time. Then knead the mixture with your hands to form a smooth dough. Shape the dough into a ball. Sprinkle the work surface with flour. Roll out the dough to just under 2.5 cm thick.

Step 3

Cut out the cookies using a cutter. Beat the remaining egg and brush it over the cookies. Sprinkle the sesame seeds on top, coating each cookie well.

Step 4

Place the cookies on the greased baking tray. Bake them in the oven for about 10 minutes.

TOP TIP Use differently shaped cookie cutters if you wish. Reduce the baking time for thin cookie shapes.

Indian Meals on the Map!

Punjab

NEW DELHI

Rajasthan

India

Chicken biryani

Lassi

Kerala

Now that you have discovered how to cook the delicious foods of India, find out where they are cooked and eaten on this map of the country.

China

Rajma

Nepal

River Ganges

West Bengal

Aloo ka paratha

Sesame cookies

Bay of Bengal

INDIAN OCEAN

29

Glossary

bazaars Indoor markets.

desert An area that has almost no rain and so has very few plants.

garnish To decorate food before serving.

Hindu Someone who practises Hinduism, a religion in India.

ingredients Different foods and seasonings that are used to make a recipe.

mosques Muslim places of worship.

mountain range An area that has many mountains.

Muslim A person who practises the Islamic faith.

pip The hard centre in the middle of some fruit that contains the seed.

quench To drink something that stops a feeling of thirst.

sauté To lightly fry food in oil or butter.

savoury Food that does not taste sweet.

seasoned Given flavour.

spices Powders that are rich in taste and are used to add flavour to food.

state An area of a country that may have its own laws.

temple A place where people go to worship.

traders People who buy and sell goods.

tribes Groups of people who live together and who have the same beliefs and ways of doing things.

tropical forests Forests with a very high rainfall.

Further Reading

India (A World of Food), Anita Ganeri, Franklin Watts

India (Looking at Countries), Jillian Powell, Franklin Watts

India (My Holiday in), Jane Bingham, Wayland

Websites

Discover more Indian recipes at:
www.vegrecipesofindia.com/recipes/kids-recipes

Learn more about India at:
www.natgeokids.com/uk/discover/geography/countries/country-fact-file-india/

Read more information at:
www.sciencekids.co.nz/sciencefacts/countries/india.html

Index